SMOTHER

SMOTHER

POEMS

Rachel Richardson

W. W. NORTON & COMPANY
Independent Publishers Since 1923

For information about permission to reproduce selections from
this book, write to Permissions, W. W. Norton & Company,
Inc., 500 Fifth Avenue, New York, NY 10110

For information about special discounts for bulk purchases, please contact
W. W. Norton Special Sales at specialsales@wwnorton.com or 800-233-4830

Manufacturing by Versa Press
Book design by Beth Steidle
Production manager: Gwen Cullen

ISBN 978-1-324-08610-9

W. W. Norton & Company, Inc., 500 Fifth Avenue, New York, NY 10110
www.wwnorton.com

W. W. Norton & Company Ltd., 15 Carlisle Street, London W1D 3BS

1 2 3 4 5 6 7 8 9 0

I automatically reject any poem
with the word "mother" in it.

—J. D. McClatchy,
editor, *The Yale Review*

CONTENTS

SMOTHER

CREEK FIRE

The dark comes in on my girl's tenth birthday.

Fire bearing crow feathers—no, ash.

It comes with its big breath,
sun without light.
                    Cold morning
in the surrounding counties,

everyone blinking, looking around,

phones lifted to the horizon.

DOMESTIC

Yesterday, as he was hacking down the passionflower vine, my husband,
whom I directed to do this, brutal creature that I have become, destroyer

of the purple-spiked flower and the fritillary's nectar, who put the power
whacker in his hands, bright orange handle so that it could not get lost

in the weeds, toothed blades, heft of gas power in the palm—yesterday,
as he was doing my bidding on a ladder against the house, gently pulling

then buzzing one tendril after another, there was a sudden cry—not
Frost's rueful laugh, not Bishop's *Oh* of pain, but the high clucking trill

of a mother squirrel as two pink bodies tumbled to the dirt. In the tangle
of shorn vines they wriggled and squeaked, hairless, blind, shining as if oiled,

as the hidden mother scolded (or so it sounded, even at her most desperate),
trilling the repeating alarm—and my husband staggered back from them,

hand over mouth, then retreated inside and returned with a box.
And I, at my great distance, trowel poised over the blueberry pots,

thought of telling him to keep it quiet so the kids wouldn't hear and angle
for a pet; I thought of having to bottle feed the things now that they'd have our

human smell, of driving them in crosstown traffic to the wildlife rescue,
of the inconvenience of their living—while my husband scooped them up

in his gentle hands, then climbed the ladder with the box and set them back
behind the green curtain of vine, in with the torn Warriors flag they'd made for
    a bed,

up against the warm wall of our house, in the nest for the mother to take them
    back,
and then waited to see if she would have them.

My mother is a moon out to sea.

It's summer. She's tired.
No one knows where she's been.

I wanted to be a good mother, the mother says.

Machine of the mother: white city inside her.

—mother we must
take away the phone because who
will you call next—

My mother would be a falconress—

My mother was the clouded-over night
a moon swims through.

She held the beginning of life.

Whatever she was to me, she was
the human caught in something she could hardly stand.

she got us almost through the high grass
then seemed like she turned around
and ran
right back in

I upload again and again
the little circles on the map
representing their air—

    (my children in their tents—)

cursing when red turns
to purple, praying to the god
I pray to, which is no god,

which is the vast smoky sky,
for orange, then yellow. Let me
be so bold as to pray

for green.

  ~

(Children in their tents are not a metaphor. The fire burning thirty
    miles away is not a metaphor.)

(What will reach them and what will not reach them is not the
    question. I am one hundred fifty miles away, 3 hours 18 minutes'
    drive time in current traffic.)

(I sit, then stand, then sit. They're probably in the rec hall now,
    playing board games so as not to tax their lungs—)

              The fire was not
considered a danger when it
ignited on a rocky hilltop, and so it was left

to burn. Wind, heat,
the big empty sky
drew a path into the forest—

By definition, a screw
is basically a nail. An inclined plane
wrapped around a nail.

Designed to mate. The male thread
wants the female thread (said
the men who named these parts), as

external and internal want
each other. Facilitated
by a nut. Or alone:

⁓

some screws are designed to cut
a helical groove into soft material.
Once a girl wandered

alone through a stand
of pines, body cutting a groove
in air. Once a woman

drove home from work.
To walk is to lay a path; to root
is to anchor. The tool is versatile,

like the coyote, solitary
or running in a pack.

～

                        They lowered
their heads at the woman
in the driveway, they between her

and her house,
lowered them so that their eyes cut,
six of them . . .

～

The common use of a screw
is to hold objects together.
What would we say held the pack

there, high on the ridge in El Cerrito?
In the middle of my neighborhood, she said.
They can be turned or driven—

～

turned or driven, until they reach
a bearing surface. A bearing surface
is often a head. It may, in this

instance, be a body.
Threaded. A bolt.

～

Another rule is this:

curl the fingers of your hand
in the direction you want the screw
to go. The woman's hand gripped the leather handle

of the bag she carried—for to hold
is to wield, and it was a weight, it might act
as a bearing surface—

～

and she skirted them, back around
to the car door and slammed
herself inside, even as two advanced

upon her.

～

The screw, in short, is any helical device:
Archimedes envisioned the threading
of one material into another by way of a plane.

To turn inward, to curl the hand, rather than
to force. That this would make a tighter bond.

~

A screw is not force but convincing.

~

The houses, anchored on the hillside,
fasten themselves to the edge of woods.
Which used to be all there was.

The coyotes don't know this in language, but
wilderness is threaded
into their bones. The woman sits

in her car at the top of the hill
in front of her house, punching the numbers
on her phone—

~

—police, fire, animal

control—as the sun melts into the bay,
its bearing surface. Pulling down the dark
like curled hands holding a blanket to the neck.

It's a cold night. A clincher.
Meanwhile, animal footsteps.
The silent fieldstones of the drive.

The empty house. The landscaping
affixed gently, with generous spacing, so as
not to overflow the plat.

FISHBOWL

Two weeks after the ordeal with the goldfish—choosing the exact pair the kids wanted and netting them among their school at the shopping center's Petco, and bagging and buying them and bringing them home, and letting the water sit, then naming them and pouring them into this world we'd made, then burying one (Fiona) in the yard, with full ceremony, and replacing her (Fiona II), and choosing the glittery blue rocks to amuse them so that their lives wouldn't only be about circling the tiny bowl on our dining room table but circling the tiny bowl *looking at something beautiful*—that's when the kids give them up.

Playing God or mother (giver of food and light, maker of beauty) has dulled. And so the fish, like orange flames, drift unnoticed within the contours of their sphere. When I think of it, I pinch flakes into their bowl. While over the crest of hills, smoke wafts toward us, and opening the door of our own glassed enclosure brings the smell of campfire, which is the burning of houses, hotels, and suburban trees fifty miles north. It's an old story, a fable we're learning to tell: another fall, another fire. Monitor the air quality sites. Switch on the purifiers, fill the bottles with water. Leave the inhaler by the bed. Pray to the gods of wind. Our bags are packed, though we know this isn't our fire. But the fire that comes for us may first send its white ash to cover our lawn like a veil, or may wake us with its hot rasp already at our necks.

~

I think how the fire will take them—the roar that will fill the rooms we humans have surrendered and burst this little globe in an explosion of sparks.

How relentless the holiness, the cataclysms—

~

The goldfish may actually have a memory, contrary to previous belief, but the science suggests it's cinematic, and at most two seconds in length, like a slideshow:

glint of dyed ultramarine pebbles // light
bending through convex glass //
flash of tail // jostle of waves

as a blurred figure bumps the table, skipping past.

WOODWARD FIRE

In some places the fire passed
lightly, searing only the west
side of the trees, crawling
through grasses.

What you know you may not know.

The field was spared and we rejoiced.
Thus endeth the first lesson.

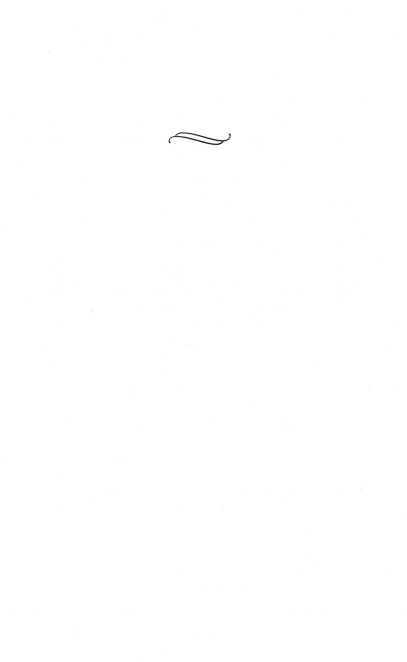

THE "I WANT" SONG

I just want them to stop emailing. All of them. You. The bots.
I want the kids to stop whining, the floor
to sweep itself, the sun to rise blamelessly
into the sky. In every movie my kids love, the main character
gets to turn, look into the camera, and howl
her "I Want" song straight into our chests.
The writers even call it that: I want
love, want to walk on two feet, want
to see the world, and yes,
I want to be queen. And once it's been laid out
for all of us to hear, we know
she has to get it.
                    But there's so much that I want—
for the trees not to burn, or at least
not *these* trees, not unless they're far away or
beneficial to the understory. I want to stop
feeling like I'd better buy the fruit
now because maybe next year there will be
no more fruit, no more water, maybe the crops will burn
or wither or be sprayed with the chemical that kills
the bees and which studies now show
kills the bees' children and children's children
two bee-generations after exposure.
I want not to think about the expiration of the world.

I want to delete my profile, want pollination
of the blossom and the swelling of fruit.
I want to stand inside the fog socked in under a crown
of redwoods. And then to become the fog.

There was a story I read, years ago, about
a tree the conservationists named Hyperion.
It was a 600-year-old coast redwood,
probably the tallest tree on earth. They wouldn't say
where it was.

                  Please don't look for it,
they said. Even footsteps will damage the root system.

A Reddit thread two months later begins with
a picture of a young smiling man, who captions it:
Here I am, standing in front of Hyperion!

And then it wasn't just plastic
at Gore Point in the Antarctic (population: 0)
but at thirty thousand feet above
the Pyrenees (population: birds)
and in the lungs of every living
lunged creature to walk
or fly or swim the planet,
and still we bought houses in the floodplain,
went to the beach when we could.
Then it wasn't a story anyone
could bear hearing again, not
with the smoke and Amazon's delay
delivering air purifiers ordered with Prime.
The people huddled
looking into their private, blue-lit screens,
trying to think of what to type
that might communicate
this leaden grief, the totality
of the body's aloneness
in which we somehow lived
together—and we believed what we believed
about who was at fault,
and it's true many things also thrived
at this time (for one must
take a balanced view): the tick and

the jellyfish flourished! And what burned
burned, and what entered
our lungs entered them silently, which
does not mean without
consequence, and then did
what it was going to do.

The news sometimes mentions the fire—new records of acres burned every day, 100,000, then 120,000—

Then back to the story of the missing girl. She's 22 but they call her a girl. Don't we know her boyfriend did it? I'm trying not to follow but I hear it every time I cross town to take my kids to circus class, and again to pick them up.

On Twitter someone posts a picture: all those tent cabins, just redwood platforms naked among the trees now that the cots and canvas and sleeping children are removed: skeletal in the haze.

I hover over the like button—not because I *like* this but I want Twitter to know I want to see more. Or maybe I don't want Twitter to know anything about me.

They spend all day with their little masks hooked to their ears, hanging their bodies upside down from silks suspended from the ceiling. They want to be circus performers, and their teacher tells them they can be.

I don't like this. I don't like anything. I push the arrow away and continue my traceless scroll.

Reporters describe the wilderness area where the girl was last seen, and the van where she lived, from which she was launching her blog. I click off the radio when the kids hop into the backseat, glitter creased in their eyelids and across their cheeks.

The Caldor Fire surrounds the summer camp where I picked them up last week, dirt-streaked and smiling.

We're following its advance on Twitter, a bunch of moms texting:

it's gone, right? all of it?

how will we tell the kids

It's been two weeks since the girl went missing. The boyfriend says he last saw her with the van. They're #vanlifers, the news explains, on a cross-country road trip to build their brand. She half-smiled in all the pictures, sleep-washed, thin pajama strap falling off her shoulder as she poured a single steaming coffee with the mountains jagged in the background. Snap. But they'd been arguing, he says. He left her with their stuff and took off for a break at home.

I brace myself to tell the kids we're about to lose their camp. They just look at me. What does that even mean? None of the images looks real.

Maybe it was animals that dragged her off, the boyfriend offers. The wolf population has been increasing in Wyoming.

In my neighborhood along the widest boulevard, 120-year-old syca-mores droop for lack of rain. Their long spindly branches hang down over passing cars like the fingers of purposeless women on a couch, having to sit there for the company. Their paper leaves, those majes-tic broad stars, wither into sick yellow.

On the girl's Instagram she said her interests were art, yoga, and veg-gies. She changed her handle three times to make it more memorable.

Announcing their engagement, she wrote: "You make my life feel unreal."

The kids jostle for space in the backseat. We drive beneath the trees, like passing under a disease.

She hit him too, the news reports. The officer says she was going to be written up for domestic violence. There were bruises on her face, but she was the one hitting him when the witness called it in. They'd been in a lovers' quarrel, he thought, or maybe she was having a men-tal break. He put down *mental break* in his notes to avoid having to bring anyone to jail.

The Caldor Fire will burn until the rains come, the reporter says.

The boyfriend is missing now. He left a note for his family saying he was going backpacking two states away. We know what this means. Don't we know what this means?

The firefighters retreated, posted on Twitter it would be a total loss, but then the fire jumped the camp, didn't singe a single cabin. My texts and everyone else's texts say the same words, use the same race-less yellow emojis to express what can't be said. We're benign little faces with tears and smiles.

can you believe it?

I can't believe it.

The girl's body, strangled, was found in Wyoming. Probably they'll find the boyfriend's body, bullet to the head, in a few weeks, and we'll understand he was overcome with guilt at what he'd done. Or he'll be gone forever, the way smoke twines upward and then just disappears, particulate in the air.

After I drop the kids, I stop by the nursery to stand among the baby plants. It's always wet and green under the canopy, everything in its little pot.

The Caldor Fire has consumed 220,000 acres and the forecast is sun, ten days of sun.

QUESTIONS

If there's one true thing, it's that
Google will make money
off us no matter what. If we want to know
what percentage of America is white
(as it seems we do)
what percentage of the population is gay
(as it seems we do)
what percentage of the earth is water:
the engine is ready for our desire.
The urgent snow is everywhere
is a line by Edna St. Vincent Millay, and
many have asked, apparently,
where am I right now. Also
when will I die. Do you love me
may be up there, generating
high cost-per-click, but not
as high as how to make pancakes,
what time is it in California.
So many things I wanted to ask you,
now that you're gone, and your texts
bounce back to me
undeliverable. Praise to
the goddess of the internet search, who returns
with her basket of grain,
67,000 helpful suggestions

to everything we request:
how to solve a Rubik's Cube,
what to do when you're bored,
how old is the earth,
how to clear cache,
what animal am I,
why do we dream,
where are you now, come back.

Nina Ellen Riggs,
1977–2017

THE WIND AND THE RAIN

In those first weeks—first
          because she was newly arrived,
                    and so the scene had reset
as unfamiliar, a blank line,
                    even though for others it was the middle
          of a project at the office
          or a round of bloodwork or simply
                    another February—in those days, weeks,
                              her first of feeling wind
on her face, and her mother's
                    (my) hand at her forehead,
                              shielding the skin from rain,
     the neighbors had mostly
                    taken down the lit balls
               that blazed in trees   from Thanksgiving
                    through the darkest days,
          and wet yellow leaves
                              clogged the gutters, slicking
          sidewalks. Someone had given
               us a fish hat,
bit of whimsy, a chartreuse
                    knit whose softness seemed right
          for someone so newly
     born, that jarring color
               and the fin
                    swaying atop her head.

She was bunched to my chest, so it swayed
                        at my heart.   Little fish,
                swept along the sidewalks of a pallid
                college town, raining and between rains.
        Then bursts of sun from breaches in
                the pillowed clouds.

Her mouth opened in an asymmetrical yawn
                            because of a paralyzed lip—
                fairly common, the doctor said,
                    and after she learns your expressions
        you'll only see it   when she cries.

Open, shut. Cry, be calmed.
                She wriggles into spring.
                The days get longer. And
probably it is here
                in the story
        that, down the street, a cluster of Nina's cells
begins to mutate,
                        though it will be another year
                before she feels the lump.

Shakespeare's fools always let us in
                        on the truth of the scene
        when the dramatic
        figures are too busy,
                        caught in their morning plans,
                suiting up in the handmaid's skirts,
writing a love note   in a disguised hand.

The way Feste, under clear skies
after the royals' double wedding, skips offstage
singing   *for the rain,*   *it raineth*
                                        every day.

Not that I'll never hear it again, your N,
soft center like a hammock
leading to the smaller n, the sigh.
Your name is the same
in five languages,
and all the women sharing it
prance around the earth, and people
call out for them:
it can't be made to sound
like keening no matter
how slowly wailed.
Your name: sweet swing of it, in-out
like a tide, and the little boats
have all been pulled in for the season.

Nina in the undergrowth. Nina

in the coffee's steam. The dead simply

don't have bodies anymore, someone

said to me. It doesn't mean they're gone.

The word horse unhorses

every other word, C.D. Wright wrote.

Say her name: the reeds move.

GYRE

The mass of the plastic in the Great Pacific Garbage Patch
was estimated to be approximately 100,000 tonnes. Once
these plastics enter the gyre, they are unlikely to leave
the area until they degrade into smaller microplastics
under the effects of sun, waves, and marine life.

—THE OCEAN CLEANUP, ANNUAL REPORT, 2020

~

circuit of current

convergence

the heart a trash collector
until the winds change

~

what floats:

Game Boy
milk crate
Rubik's Cube

~

the heart a deep quiet

under the sun
a disintegration zone

within its circuit of current
spiraling by—

~

Walkman
bobblehead
rubber duck

~

convergence

the heart of a picker

scooping her treasures
then breaking them down
to component parts

~

Nerf gun
juice box
ghost net

~

divergence

spits it all out
back to the circuit

the spiral
the crack   the whip end

expelling her debris

for its travels

~

it means nothing
is no one

~

red balloon and its ribbon . . .

~

what it kills, it kills

44

The dog scratches.
The neighbor pulls his trash bin
up from the curb.
I sit in the dark, not wanting to be found.
Why is the child crying in this poem,
you ask? You wonder
is the mother a bad mother,
is the child hurt or sick, or
is it just to say this is a
Mother Poem, choosing its audience
because the author, who is the mother,
needs a friend to say You still
have a brain, You write poems!,
Your child is fine she'll be fine
she'll never remember when she's
your age how you yelled at her
to shut up after the question
that had only two answers, yes or no,
kept getting answered
neither. It's the wailing,
the grievance, like a knife
into the ear, that shapes
the poem—I'm sorry, I'm trying
to hear another kind of music
but thinking only of discordant
things like the gymnastics coach

who killed himself—just
monstrous enough to aid in the abuse
of the other coach, the one
whose name we all know, but not
monstrous enough to feel
no remorse. Or maybe
it was only fear he felt. He'd been caught.
I'm monstrous too, though, writing
my poem with this wailing in the background
that doesn't stop, hasn't stopped,
and wanting someone to pity me
because the argument was about
whether she'd allow me to remove
her Band-Aid which she wanted removed
but didn't. And I didn't
consider, didn't wait
for a turn, or quiet myself to hear
under her wailing
another rhythm. I am not
always here for the life
of the poem. Sometimes what I want
is absolute power, sometimes
I want to pick up
her little body and set her down
in a desert like the ancient gods
did to the infidels, and watch
her eyes widen at the expanse
of dunes and dry heat. But she was
screaming in the narrow
bathroom and I could only

look at my own face
three ways in the mirror, white
tile gleaming everywhere
behind us, so I reached
down, took her in my talons
and tore the bandage from her arm.

Held in books, in flesh, in the thread that binds me to those who are also putting a child to bed, slicing a potato, pulling to the side of the highway to change a tire.

There you are, my friend across the abyss. Your generalized body now, unhorsed: the fog that catches, sometimes, here, between the rolling hills.

Montaigne said (I know you know this)
No art can achieve likeness. And even though
it seems he changed his mind many times
a day and had no problem contradicting
his own claims, I think we believe this one.

Right, Nina? It's true. Nothing I'm making
revives you.

LIGHTNING COMPLEX

The good idea
burned

is what
they're saying:

glittering possibility
like a bridge

painted orange
in welcome, or

the dazzle
of lights stringing

the coast.
You can

see it from
space. And

one day
if you think

long enough
beyond

yourself,
it's gone.

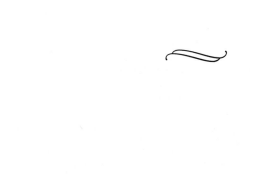

SMOTHER

The smoke never appears in family pictures.

The smoke got up this morning and ran a marathon. She came in first in her age group without trying.

The smoke's children are fine, just where they should be on the growth chart. She lets their father cut their hair.

The smoke writes her novels in the bath.

She's cool with school lunch.
Her Twitter is a thing of beauty.
Her kids are her inspiration.

The smoke cherishes each moment. She doesn't nag about people leaving the lights on. She just steps over the shoes by the door.

The smoke is a statue. She's the life of the party.

The smoke gets it all done and is happily exhausted in the evening. She can laugh at that joke—*exhausted*.

The smoke didn't have to leave home to write about it.

And what about the epics? She exhales. The smoke has an inner life, but it's the same as her outer life.

The smoke has gone to Boston. To Cameroon. To Siberia. She doesn't believe in *Go back to where you came from*. She has no use for *Isn't that a bit ambitious*.

The smoke knows she changes everything. Yellows the light on the lake. Smears out the trees.

The smoke has heard it all before.

When given the option she'll take the stairs. She gets 10,000 steps before most people are awake. She's never been tired a day in her life.

The smoke was bored with the adjunct track, so she went and got an MBA.

Who gets to transform is a material concern, but it's also a question of attitude. When people say "she has boss energy," they're talking about the smoke.

The smoke is a wrestler, a runner, a woman with a basket of fruit. No. The smoke is something else now. There's no keeping up with her.

She knows seeing ain't believing. The lake and the mountain are only the idea of a lake and a mountain. Her motto is: Life is what you make it.

She doesn't worry about her skin or her weight or what she said to the hiring committee. The smoke does not *dwell*. She certainly doesn't check her email 30 times a day.

The smoke believes in her aspirational applications: biomass into biochar. Biochar to feed the soil. Waste plastics into usable oil.

The smoke is all about growth mindset. She always has more of herself to give.

Her favorite game is close your eyes and count to ten.

The smoke rolls in and rolls out. She doesn't care about summer camp or swimming in the lake.

Of course she says one thing when she means another. The smoke loves a good metaphor. What remains in its place on earth, anchored in its own skin?

One minute she's your grandmother with her sweating rocks glass in the parlor. Then she's the crow on the telephone line.

The smoke has never taken a day for granted.

Fake it 'til you make it is an attitude she can respect.

And what will you do for the smoke? What can you give her that she doesn't already have? She moves, and stays, and moves, and enters. Every surface is permeable for the smoke.

The smoke thinks it's funny that you remember her orange gray haze, that this memory means something to you. You are not her, not in your wildest dreams.

Though you too are made of particulate. You too are made of millions of burning trees.

And how would you know yourself if not inside that blur? That smothering of the terrible sun?

The smoke is not cruel, only truthful.

The smoke might be a result of the patriarchy, but the smoke is not the patriarchy. Correlation is not causation. You of all people should know that.

The smoke is a natural consequence. She is awake to the mountains fleshed with trees, the houses made of boards. Her fingers feel for entry; she knows how to warp and curl.

She knows warp and curl are the only movements on earth; straight lines are the fantasy of your kind. She goes high and low, circumvents your brace-and-bolt, your Simpson ties. Your love for naming things after yourselves, as if this binds your little dwellings to earth.

But earth is soil; the worms carry it. Earth is rock and gas, which churn.

The smoke loves her mother. She doesn't slink around looking for credit for each little favor she performs; she doesn't demand to be treated like a professional while eating Cheetos in her sweatpants on Zoom.

The smoke doesn't sit with her feelings.

Air or no air, she grows.

The smoke has had enough of your bullshit.

The smoke doesn't mutter, doesn't get into one-upping her own kid. She slips across highways, lakes, nestles in hillsides. But the smoke doesn't love them. She doesn't want your offerings. So what that you know her name.

You dress too sloppy. You can be swayed by the smallest desire. Just one drink and you'll stay.

The smoke goes where she goes. Double-booking is fine. She believes in bootstraps, in the charismatic leader. Somebody's got to get things done.

Stop asking who you'd be without her. The smoke doesn't want you any more than she wants anything. You're a lesser fuel, an object in a field.

Shut down your machine, your little wheel.

The smoke has enough children of her own.

TELEPHONE

Warm movement
on skin, voice
brought inside
my ear
as if through
that cord I
used to weave
around my index
finger, ring
finger, across wrists to
cuff me to its
sound, its intelligible
replication of the human
voice. The patent:
device that can fuse
across space
when two are
too far
apart to be heard
directly. I twined
that cord to my
arms, wrapped
myself within
the sound.
Speak. And assemble

the parts that bring her:
transmitter/
receiver/
ringer. My daughter,
unknower
of the telephone,
cups her
hand against
my ear, whispers
a sentence, chain
I am supposed
not to break but pass
unharmed through
my body to
another ear and
across until
it comes back to her—
replication,
microphone,
earphone—delivered
unto her
body by warm
breath fogging
the ear—
and its mangled
arrival, heap
of syllables
ruptured and
bent out

of order,
everyone so near
and laughing
now at
how far
how indirectly
the replication imagined
what she said.

SHUTDOWN

Goodbye to the dinner party,
to the mosh pit, goodbye
hand I don't recognize on the small
of my back. Goodbye let me hold that
for you, and goodbye teenaged babysitters,
the girl with razor scars on her arms
and the one in the crop top, all juniors
at Berkeley High. Goodbye big kid offering
a hand up into the tree, the thick
gnarl of the coast oak that is illegal
to cut. Goodbye moms, elbow to elbow
in the bar. Goodbye bar. Goodbye quiet
of the shutting door, goodbye school bells
three blocks away. Goodbye coffeeshop
hoverer waiting for my table, goodbye couch
I shared with a stranger. Goodbye stringy-haired boy
and goodbye dreadlocked boy and goodbye boy
with the frat-basement-shaved head. Goodbye boys
who believed they were no longer
boys. Goodbye girl with the nose pierce,
FAFSA app, with untied
white Nikes. Goodbye says the teacher
on the video line, and the first grader whispers
to her classmates as they log off
one by one, "bye, bye,
bye, bye, bye . . ."

They're jewels, delivered
by a sister I don't touch.
Eggs, in a plastic
carton, fitted into
their dozen plastic settings:
a bracelet, two
by two. Left on a ledge
because these days
the touch of skin,
the sharing of air—
we don't.
But the dog noses out
of the screen door
before it wheezes shut
behind me with my bounty, and
prances down the front steps, wagging, into
the abandoned street.

We're passing the Hollingsworth Fulfillment Center, big box wedged between the fields and trailers, then paved lots of rebar and mulch, cedar boards being showered under sprinklers, awaiting use in construction. We're passing a treeless mobile home development named Almond Groves.

Sometimes, after the heroine's desire song is sung, she doesn't get what she wants. Then she sings it again but in anger. Writers call this the Dark Reprise. There's no escaping her want, and what she might do to grasp it.

We cross over the North Fork of the Tuolumne River, then over again, bisecting its curve, on our way down the mountain where we planted incense cedars and big leaf maples to cover the Rim Fire's scar.

In the flats, we pass Century Communities, 55+, now selling: half-built houses spreading across fields facing the highway.

The kids want to talk to Siri, want their own Alexa, a woman waiting to answer every desire.

I watch for a place to pull over and collect mistletoe so that we can hang it in doorways and make the kids gag when we ambush them with kisses—they're old enough to hate it and that makes me want it more.

We have to spot it in a live oak outside a fence line, low enough to reach. I can see the balls of it hovering, but it's too high in the near branches, only low in the trees far into someone's pasture: the yellow-green tinge of it thriving as it siphons nutrients from the tree. I crane my neck. Tell my husband: drive slow, get ready to swerve off the road.

If you love a forest, you're supposed to live in a small house. Accept your grandmother's hand-me-down sewing rocker instead of snatching up the sectional at the liquidation sale.

You need to learn about soil and beetles, heart rot and the price of lumber in China.

Turns out the world is not the silence under a crown of redwoods, not mostly.

The builders are always building. Zillow hungers for a listing. Treed lots photograph so beautifully, framing the dappled light.

If you want a forest you should buy the trees. If you want a forest you should deed them to the conservationists to keep from your descendants' desires.

Turns out the price of lumber in China is going up up up. It's not productive to love a thing that costs so much to keep in the ground. The loggers are waiting. The local economy is counting on you.

You need to lie down in the understory, to burrow and root.

A tree party is swallowing smoke. A tree party is reaching toward the sun. A tree party takes years to get to cocktail hour.

It's not your fault you loved to run your hand along smooth floor-boards as a child; it's not your fault you took the sweet air for granted.

Still, bereft, something in me wants to sing
but without words: the throat opening
to make its O.

The greens of palms shuddering in the rain.

The pooling water silvering even the parking lot.

Rainbow of oil lengthening into a crescent.

And my feet,
snapped into spikes below my running shoes
in another weather system entirely,
acknowledge the ice
of the farm road as I run crunching—

lucky, lucky—the smoke of my breath and

the huddled sheep, off-white

against the white hill in the dazzling sun—

This is weeks ago
already. We are people

who fly, who can live among palms and snowdrifts
concurrently, who can live
alone (O, alone).

And here comes the banjo again,
that one repeated riff, fingers
moving up and down the frets:
I never meant to leave
the key out for any taker, but I'm so easy sometimes
with my heart

      —O to close

my eyes. To hear it rise.

GIRL FRIEND POEM:

Nomi

It's the tree I can't get over—
      salvaged Christmas tree someone hauled in
           in January,   still up mid-March, in a cabin
in Vermont, a demure circle
           of needles shed to the floor.   No one
      thought to move it, all of us swishing past
           with backpacks, pizza boxes, me
with my mixtapes stacked on the windowsill, loving a throwback
           even then—   and the earth outside
      taking its cues from the crocuses,
the thaw beginning far below the snow.

Once we saw a bear scuttle up a tree
           in the neighborhood and it took us
      three minutes to turn to each other and say
           that was a bear?

What I loved about the mixtape   was how the order
           of its songs became a message, and wherever
      it cut off was where the story had to end—
instrumental interlude or
           middle of a sentence—

You were mine among woodsmoke
        and calculus homework   (someone else's,
spilled under the couch like a paper river),   among
                        cowboy hats, let's have a sleepover,
        symmetry of bodies,

are you going to put this in a poem?

        Girl in snow boots, girl in sequins,

my new philosophy is everything goes   in a poem.

        And one day our roommates dragged that tree
into the woods and lit it—
                        galaxy of sparks in the dark forest,   our
breath steaming as we circled the flames

smoke tumbling into messages we couldn't read
        or look away from—

Lyrae

You haven't been back
to the fire-carved
landscape, manzanita clawing its way
between rocks, a dead trunk
of a mountain pine
clinging to its living
twin, tiny pink succulents clustered
at a rock seam. To
your Jeffrey pines—made
yours by your rapture
at their smell.
The granite rises like
a bowl around the lake (Echo)
and voices carry from the water
hundreds of feet below.
When did everyone
start to feel so far away?
This dry wind's ominous, the aspen leaves
anxiously fluttering, gathering
the light, fluttering.
Remember those trees by
the highway, straighter than the rest,
standing a bit aloof?
One day we realized

they were cell towers.
I never know anymore
what anyone is thinking.
Tell me again
about the hundred-year-old apple trees
on the land you bought
outside of town. Tell me how it smells
in fall. Tell me about the rain.

The 06 female gets
collared and tracked,
and her pack
sets out in search of elk.
She doesn't know
she has crossed
our invisible line.
The ranger who put the
dart between her
shoulder blades
can't bear watching
her little blinking
GPS marker glide
across his screen
with her babies in tow
out of Yellowstone
toward the hunters.
He wishes he'd
never found her.
I hear him on the radio
being interviewed
as I drive up the hill
toward our own
conservation area,
what we call the Wildland

Urban Interface, domain
of the mountain lion,
coyote, and three-
million-dollar mansions.
My shoes are laced
for my usual loop.
She was an exceptional
mother, he says.
His voice hollows
with grief, knowing
everything is in our reach.

Within that vast
triangle, land that appears
to be hanging only by a flimsy hinge
to the continent, the burn scars
having leveled the grasses, having pushed
the elk elsewhere up the ragged edge
for reeds, the hearts of some downed trees
still smolder. This is what I go for. To walk inside it,
to know what remains of the kingdom.

SMOKE CENTO

The smoke wades through black jade.

Smoke knows why the caged bird sings.

Everyone forgets the smoke also flew.

The smoke, too, sings America.

The smoke is elegy to what it signifies.

Smoke is the thing with feathers.

Smoke loved the earth so much
she wanted to stay forever.

The smoke diverged in a yellow wood.

Smoke kept us warm, covering
earth in forgetful snow . . .

But I know, too,
That the smoke is involved
In what I know.

AUTHENTICATE

I'm not a robot, I tell my computer
again and again, to be given the key
to see any sky I want
to see.

                And it,
my robot, lets me drift
in bright blue, in a landscape that
never burns, that saturates my eyes.

GIRL FRIEND POEM:

Renee

When we had no school   we made a school,
maps and Senate contests pasted on my wall   and the timeline of American history
the way we wanted it told   on yours. The kids walked between

our houses and you made bean soup   and I made yogurt and we delivered
them by child courier, your day   or my day to be teacher, and you yelled

at the kids and I yelled at the kids   and we apologized. And I forget which
one of us thought up a whole new currency   to teach them economics

and whose day was the day   the sky stayed orange and we broke into
the school playground because   breathing smoke on the monkey bars
was worth it—

And we read about Ma Ingalls   on the prairie
in seven months of winter   and little Kamala Harris
integrating our kids' own school   and we tried to remember

our luck in the world   as you made sourdough
or I did and I made leaf etchings   or you did and we packed the kids
into the van to the beach   to get off-grid when the election came.

We camped among the shorn   native grasses, mowed flat to prevent
wildfire, by the cold ocean   and we didn't know how the votes

were being tallied   and who would run the country and sign bills
into law and how those laws   would treat our children's
small bodies   and our own.

Then all our flashlights died   and the dark
came down fast   but the kids stayed in the ocean
until last light, their clothes   plastered to their skin in saltwater

and sand until they delivered themselves   to us expecting us to peel them free
and find them something dry   (our own clothes off our bodies)

and build a fire and bring them to it   and then lie on top
of the picnic table in our sleeping bags   and identify the stars

and you did   or I did   or we named enough
possible constellations with confidence   that the kids believed we knew.

And our nylon tents were our den   and our children tumbled and bit
and we wanted school back   and these creatures out of the house

and you know all these things   as well as I do
but we are forgetting already   and that's why I'm saying this,
I'm writing it down   because if you and I know anything

we know it goes.

DESPITE

after Hikmet/O'Hara/Reeves/Vuong/Rader/Wright

Today I love everything: the packed-up pack
by the door, the dry mountain,
the air I don't understand—

it's an open blueness,
crisp, as if mouths had never
breathed into it, only trees breathed out.

The silk underbark of the manzanitas gleams
after fire, the grasses first to return to green.

They lay a carpet. Everyone says this.
Even in a silent house I hear everyone
saying this.

Today I started with
a poet's poem that had derived its love
from four others

as if we all need someone else's declaration
to find our own selves—

No.
Today I started with the sun.

My skin here would become like the
manzanitas: I'd grow into

myself, I'd accept my trunk
like Daphne, I'd learn
to stretch in it, be peeled back

by flame. Smolder.
Lift my scent in the rains.

The smell of the wind is what
I am after—I don't mind
hearing the highway behind it.

Today I love everything:

the silk of my dry hair blowing,
the pickup truck on the ridge.

The sun hasn't reached my feet . . .

I like the way
the trail is carved right to the edge
of the hillside so I can feel I might
tumble off at any step

and the poison oak, glossy
from the rain, parades its beautiful leaves
toward my ankles.

Of all of us it knows
most firmly what it loves—

GIRL FRIEND POEM:

Giulia

We both stare at the sun—
no, below it, into coffee mugs.

For you the fires were the guide:
a ridge makes a red line

through the night,   you told me.
It teaches you where you have to go.

You'd watch it from your sleeping bag

with the boys on the hill,
all of you ready to deploy.   You called it

working fire—you worked fire
every summer, and the boys

who loved it most became
Hotshots, parachuting themselves

into the flame. Sometimes you'd make out
with them on the hillside as you watched its creep.

You're mine

because our children are elsewhere,
whole cities away.   You're mine

because once we lived
almost in each other's bodies,

tramping down 18th Street in pajamas.
We recorded nothing of that life,   not the sound

of the grocery truck unloading,
not the heat until we couldn't take

any more into our skin.

For you the fires were the guide.
For me, language:

I tried to grasp,
to make a pattern.

It teaches you where you have to go.

There's too much heat already—

even before breakfast   I have to wear
sunglasses in the dining room.

We weren't counting miles when we ran together
down the windy Great Highway

behind the sand dunes. . . .

Remind me I don't need it back.

Remind me—these green trees, oaks still leafing,
don't yet smell like their burning.

The kids cradled baby trees
in their arms—plastic conical pots
with the starts of incense cedars
and ponderosas sprouting upward—
tiny shivers of needles
spurting from thin beginnings
of branch—and we trudged
up the hillside with paper packets
of nutrients, tree tea, stuffed
in our jeans pockets, to toss
into the planting holes. The rains
were coming. Everything felt lucky.
We shuddered in the cold clear
air, like saplings, our fingers
numbing in flimsy garden gloves.
The camp's engineer shouted
instructions to our assembled group:
Space them six feet apart
all over the hill. To feed
the roots, scavenge
for biochar left from the burn.
Mulch them in a blanket of leaves
to protect from the early snows.
The kids carried trowels; we
parents dug and pierced orange flags

into the dirt at the planting sites
to mark our labor, the starts
of new sprouts, this imagined
shade for our children's
children. We stood over them, mothers
over young, gods for our brief moment,
remembering the engineer had said
it's reasonable to hope
that a few might make it.

CALIFORNIA FIRE MAP

Below are descriptions of the fires discussed in this book.

The Rim Fire burned 257,314 acres, which made it California's third largest wildfire at the time. It began on August 17, 2013, and was contained on October 24, 2013, but, due to lack of winter rains, it was not fully extinguished for over a year, until November 4, 2014. The Rim Fire burned the City of Berkeley's beloved family camp, Tuolumne Camp, to the ground. The camp was rebuilt in 2022 and its land reforested with saplings planted by local families. During my family's visit in summer 2022, the camp's 100th anniversary and celebrated reopening, the area was threatened again, this time by the Oak Fire.

The Woodward Fire burned 4,929 acres at Point Reyes National Seashore from August 8 to September 30, 2020.

The Creek Fire burned 379,895 acres mostly in the Sierra National Forest, from September 4 to December 24, 2020. It became the third largest California wildfire on record, until the Dixie Fire burned nearly three times its acreage the following year.

LNU, CZU, SCU, and August Complex Fires were four massive fire complexes caused by the merging of hundreds of smaller fires started by a thunderstorm. A total of 376 known fires ignited from more than 10,000 lightning strikes on August 16 and 17, 2020 in eighteen counties around the Bay Area and rural northern California, including in two old-growth redwood preserves. The fires were completely contained in October 2020, but some redwoods in Big Basin Redwoods State Park continued to smolder into 2021. In total the August 2020 Lightning Complex fires burned about 1,880,000, nearly 2% of the state of California.

The Tamarack Fire burned 68,637 acres in Alpine County from July 4, 2021, until containment on October 8, 2021.

The Caldor Fire burned 221,835 acres in the Sierra Nevada from August 14, 2021, until containment on October 21, 2021. The Caldor Fire burned up to the edge of the City of Berkeley's youth wilderness camp, Echo Lake Camp, including spot fires igniting on the property, but miraculously did not burn it down.

In the decade since the Rim Fire in 2013, the record for largest fire in California has been broken nine times.

ACKNOWLEDGMENTS

This book is for Nina Ellen Riggs (1977–2017), and for all my living women friends.

Many thanks to my early readers Nomi Stone, Mira Rosenthal, Kelly Richardson, and Elaina Ellis. For moral support in the dark days, my thanks to Renee Jansen, Chris McKnett, Anne Beatty, Giulia Good Stefani, Tiffany Schrader-Brown, Lisa Beth Anderson, Sara Houghteling, John Duberstein, Matthew Zapruder, Chris Feliciano Arnold, Cleopatra Mathis, Brenda Hillman, and Linda Gregerson. To the ladies of the ridiculous chat thread that pulled me through the pandemic: Arthi Reddy, Clara Veniard, Kelly Fisher, Lubna Ammar, Melissa Miranda, Swathi Reddy, and Karin Goodfellow. Thanks to the Left Margin LIT writing crew for making me write again after Nina's death. And to the spirits of Eavan Boland and Ken Fields, mentors always.

Deepest gratitude also to Jill Bialosky for believing in this book, and to Laura Mucha, Gabby Nugent, and all the wonderful people at Norton for bringing it into being. And most of all to David Roderick and our kids, for giving me endless material and the faith and time to work with it.

NOTES

The epigraph for this book was spoken by J. D. McClatchy in a publishing Q&A session at the Sewanee Writers' Conference in 2009 and is reproduced here from my notes at that event. I hope it is verbatim, but if not, it's close. He went further in his denunciation of mother poems in his classes at Yale, apparently; his screeds are immortalized in a profile in *The New Yorker* ("J. D. McClatchy's Poetry Lessons," by Alexandra Schwartz, April 11, 2018). I thank him for giving me a wall to push against.

Mother Cento: Lines are from poems by Saeed Jones, Dorianne Laux, Hayan Charara, Louise Glück, Jorie Graham, Robert Duncan, Reginald Shepherd, Zbigniew Herbert [translated by John and Bogdana Carpenter], Sharon Olds, and Lucille Clifton.

Lightning Complex: The title refers to the CZU, SCU, LNU, and August Lightning Complex Fires, a group of hundreds of fires started in California by lightning strikes in a rare summer thunderstorm.

Smother: Section V borrows its line "[   ] is not cruel, only truthful," from Sylvia Plath.

My "Girl Friend Poems" owe a debt to C. D. Wright, as does this whole book. She is the presiding spirit and guide to deep friendship, grief, and the language in which to say it ("in a word, a world"). In particular, I have borrowed titles and direction from Wright's "Girl Friend Poem" series in *Tremble* (Ecco, 1996). These poems are for Nomi Stone, Lyrae Van Clief-Stefanon, Renee Jansen, and Giulia Good Stefani.

Smoke Cento: In this play on a cento, the word "smoke" substitutes for other nouns in canonical poems. The poem employs lines from Marianne Moore, Maya Angelou, Jack Gilbert, Langston Hughes, Emily Dickinson, Robert Hass, Stanley Kunitz, Robert Frost, T. S. Eliot, and Wallace Stevens.

Despite: This poem is the result of what has become a popularly shared and growing poetry correspondence. Arising as a response to Frank O'Hara's "Katy," Roger Reeves and Ocean Vuong wrote poems ("Someday I'll Love Roger Reeves," "Someday I'll Love Ocean Vuong") to which Dean Rader added the influence of Nazim Hikmet's "Things I Didn't Know I Loved" and then responded ("I Never Knew I Loved Dean Rader"). My own response is to all of the earlier writers. I also add C. D. Wright to this cauldron of influence for my poem, especially for the line "the smell of the wind is what/I am after," which adapts a phrase of hers from *Cooling Time.*

After Fire: This poem refers to an event at Berkeley's Tuolumne Camp, a public family wilderness camp near Yosemite that burned to the ground in the 2013 Rim Fire. Thanks to the Friends of Berkeley Tuolumne Camp for hosting the tree planting and inspiring this poem on our collective effort.

CREDITS

Many of these poems first appeared in the following publications:

Academy of American Poets'
Poem-A-Day: "Questions"

Alta Journal: "Girl Friend Poem: Lyrae"

American Poetry Review: "Smother,"
"Elegy to the Sound of Your Name"

Cherry Tree: "Caldor Fire"

Copper Nickel: "Approximate
Distance," "Nina Redux"

The Greensboro Review: "Undeliverable"

Ecotone: "Zeitgeist"

The Florida Review: "Gyre," "Permission"

Hunger Mountain: "Fishbowl,"
"Girl Friend Poem: Giulia"

The Missouri Review: "Conservation Theory," "The 'I Want' Song," "Shutdown," "The Wind and the Rain"

NELLE: "Girl Friend Poem: Nomi," "Poem with Child Crying in the Background"

Orion Magazine: "After Fire"

Public School Poetry: "Authenticate," "Despite," "Lightning Complex," "Smoke Cento"

San Francisco Chronicle: "Contactless Delivery"

Terrain.org: "Creek Fire," "Fulfillment," "Tamarack Fire," "The Map Is Not the Territory," "Woodward Fire"

West Marin Review: "Familiar Melody"

The Yale Review: "The Houses Anchored on the Hillside"

"The 'I Want' Song" was also featured in the podcast "The Slowdown," hosted by Major Jackson.